CREEPY CRAWLIES
Scorpions

by Kari Schuetz

BELLWETHER MEDIA · MINNEAPOLIS, MN

Note to Librarians, Teachers, and Parents:

Blastoff! Readers are carefully developed by literacy experts and combine standards-based content with developmentally appropriate text.

Level 1 provides the most support through repetition of high-frequency words, light text, predictable sentence patterns, and strong visual support.

Level 2 offers early readers a bit more challenge through varied simple sentences, increased text load, and less repetition of high-frequency words.

Level 3 advances early-fluent readers toward fluency through increased text and concept load, less reliance on visuals, longer sentences, and more literary language.

Level 4 builds reading stamina by providing more text per page, increased use of punctuation, greater variation in sentence patterns, and increasingly challenging vocabulary.

Level 5 encourages children to move from "learning to read" to "reading to learn" by providing even more text, varied writing styles, and less familiar topics.

Whichever book is right for your reader, Blastoff! Readers are the perfect books to build confidence and encourage a love of reading that will last a lifetime!

This edition first published in 2016 by Bellwether Media, Inc.

No part of this publication may be reproduced in whole or in part without written permission of the publisher. For information regarding permission, write to Bellwether Media, Inc., Attention: Permissions Department, 5357 Penn Avenue South, Minneapolis, MN 55419.

Library of Congress Cataloging-in-Publication Data

Schuetz, Kari, author.
  Scorpions / by Kari Schuetz.
    pages cm. – (Blastoff! Readers. Creepy Crawlies)
    Summary: "Developed by literacy experts for students in kindergarten through grade three, this book introduces scorpions to young readers through leveled text and related photos"– Provided by publisher.
  Audience: Ages 5-8
  Audience: K to grade 3
Includes bibliographical references and index.
  ISBN 978-1-62617-226-5 (hardcover: alk. paper)
  1. Scorpions–Juvenile literature. I. Title.
  QL458.7.S38 2016
  595.4'6–dc23
                        2015002651

Printed in the United States of America, North Mankato, MN.

Table of Contents

Quite a Grip

Scorpions are **arachnids** with a strong grip.

They have large claws. These crush **insects**, spiders, and other **prey**.

claws

Helpful Hairs

Scorpions have hairy legs. These help find prey.

9

The hairs brush
the ground.
They feel other
animals move.

A Sting to It

Every scorpion has a **stinger**. This protects against **predators**.

stinger

The stinger also shoots **venom** into prey. Then the animal stops moving.

The scorpion breaks down its prey. It slurps up the food.

Out of Sight

Scorpions live in hot and cold places. They often stay in **burrows** or under rocks.

They can hide
for months
without food!

Glossary

arachnids—small animals with eight legs and hard outer bodies; an arachnid's body is divided into two parts.

burrows—holes or tunnels that some animals dig in the ground

insects—small animals with six legs and hard outer bodies; an insect's body is divided into three parts.

predators—animals that hunt other animals for food

prey—animals that are hunted by other animals for food

stinger—a body part that shoots poison

venom—a poison

To Learn More

AT THE LIBRARY

Bodden, Valerie. *Scorpions*. Mankato, Minn.: Creative Education, 2011.

Emberley, Rebecca. *The Crocodile and the Scorpion*. New York, N.Y.: Roaring Brook Press, 2013.

Ganeri, Anita. *Scorpion*. Chicago, Ill.: Heinemann Library, 2011.

ON THE WEB

Learning more about scorpions is as easy as 1, 2, 3.

1. Go to www.factsurfer.com.

2. Enter "scorpions" into the search box.

3. Click the "Surf" button and you will see a list of related web sites.

With factsurfer.com, finding more information is just a click away.

Index

The images in this book are reproduced through the courtesy of: Marco Uliana, front cover; Peter Bay, p. 5; Bruce Coleman, Inc./ Alamy, p. 7; Milan Vachal, p. 9; davemhuntphotography, p. 11; Juan Martinez, p. 13 (scorpion); raulbaenacasado, p. 13 (roadrunner); Biosphoto/ SuperStock, p. 15; Minden Pictures/ SuperStock, p. 17; Tony Phelps/ Nature Picture Library, p. 19; NHPA/ SuperStock, p. 21.